ALFRED NOBLE LIBRARY
32901 Plymouth Rd
Livonia, MI 48150-1793
] (734) 421-6600

LIVN #19

EXPANSION OF OUR NATION

THE INDIAN REMOVAL ACT AND THE
TRAIL OF TEARS

by Susan E. Hamen

ALFRED NOBLE LIBRARY
32901 Plymouth Rd
Livonia, MI 48150-1793
(734) 421-6600

FOCUS
READERS

OCT 17 2018

3 9082 13655 2091

WWW.FOCUSREADERS.COM

Copyright © 2019 by Focus Readers, Lake Elmo, MN 55042. All rights reserved. No part of this book may be reproduced or utilized in any form or by any means without written permission from the publisher.

Focus Readers is distributed by North Star Editions:
sales@northstareditions.com | 888-417-0195

Produced for Focus Readers by Red Line Editorial.

Content Consultant: Dr. Gideon Mailer, Associate Professor of History, University of Minnesota Duluth

Photographs ©: Picture History/Newscom, cover, 1; North Wind Picture Archives, 4–5, 6, 10–11, 13, 15, 16–17, 19, 21; Red Line Editorial, 9, 26; John T. Bowen/Lithographic & Print Colouring Establishment/Library of Congress, 23; JFLO217, 24–25; JNix/Shutterstock Images, 29

ISBN
978-1-63517-881-4 (hardcover)
978-1-63517-982-8 (paperback)
978-1-64185-185-5 (ebook pdf)
978-1-64185-084-1 (hosted ebook)

Library of Congress Control Number: 2018931683

Printed in the United States of America
Mankato, MN
May, 2018

ABOUT THE AUTHOR

Susan E. Hamen has written more than 30 books for children on a wide variety of topics. Her book *Clara Barton: Civil War Hero and American Red Cross Founder* was chosen for the ALA's 2011 Amelia Bloomer Project Book List. Hamen lives in Minnesota with her husband, daughter, and son.

TABLE OF CONTENTS

CHAPTER 1

A GRAB FOR LAND

After the United States gained its independence from Great Britain, the young nation was eager to expand. Many US citizens wanted land they could settle and farm. Some moved west beyond the Appalachian Mountains. Others moved to Georgia and other parts of the American South. These areas had rich farmland.

Hundreds of American Indian tribes lived in North America long before the United States existed.

Thousands of Seminoles lived in Florida during the late 1700s and early 1800s.

During the late 1700s, settlers rushed to claim the land as their own.

But the land was not empty. American Indian nations had lived there for many years. They included the Cherokees, Creeks, Choctaws, Chickasaws, and Seminoles. The settlers tried to force these American Indian nations off the land. They built more and more farms and houses. Soon, fighting broke out as American Indians tried to defend their homelands.

Some American Indian nations tried to make peace. In November 1785, Cherokee leaders met with US **representatives**. They signed the **Treaty** of Hopewell. This agreement created boundaries between the Cherokees' land and the settlers' land. If settlers were found on the Cherokees' land, the Cherokees could force the settlers to leave.

Even so, settlers kept moving onto Cherokee land anyway. Soon, hundreds of families lived illegally on Cherokee land.

US President George Washington did not think he could force the settlers to leave. Instead, he supported **acculturation**. Cherokees were pressured to **convert** to Christianity. They were taught to speak and read English. Five American Indian nations in the southeastern United States adopted these practices. Still, this did not bring peace. Settlers wanted more land.

On July 2, 1791, Cherokee leaders signed another treaty with the United States. They believed this treaty would bring lasting peace between them and the settlers. Known as the Treaty of Holston, it set up new boundaries for the Cherokees' land. As part of the treaty, more land was sold to the United States. Many Cherokees gave up their traditional ways of life. They stopped hunting. Instead, they settled in one place. Many became successful farmers. However, the peace did not last long.

TRADITIONAL AMERICAN INDIAN HOMELANDS

CHEROKEE TERRITORY

CHICKASAW TERRITORY

ATLANTIC OCEAN

CHOCTAW TERRITORY

CREEK TERRITORY

N
W E
S

SEMINOLE TERRITORY

GULF OF MEXICO

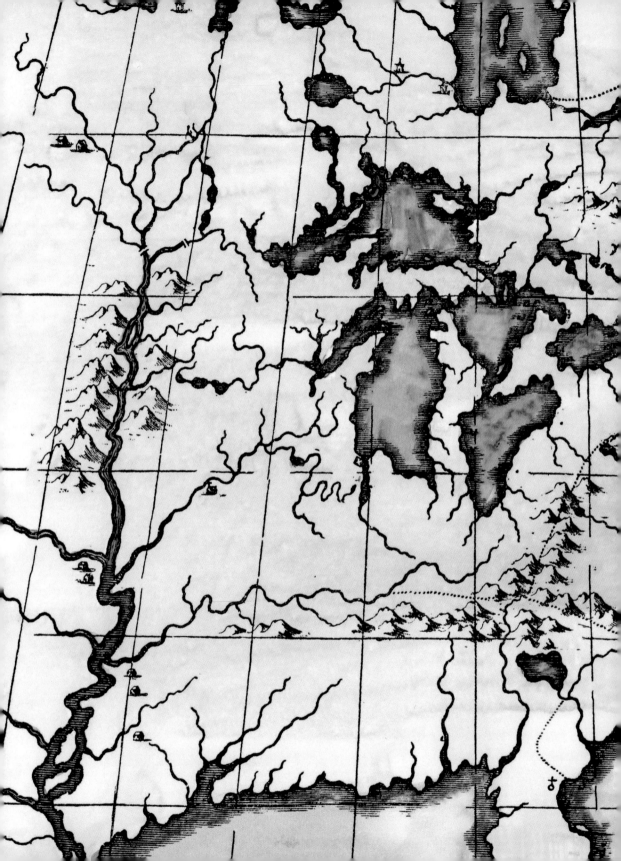

CHAPTER 2

THE INDIAN REMOVAL ACT

In 1794, the Cherokees formed the National **Council**. No Cherokee land could be sold without permission from this group. Thomas Jefferson became US president in 1801. He hoped the Cherokees would be willing to sell more of their land. But they were not. So, US lawmakers made plans to take it.

US settlers wanted to move past the Appalachian Mountains to land that belonged to native nations.

Jefferson signed the Georgia Compact in 1802. In this agreement, Georgia agreed to sell its western lands to the US government. In exchange, Jefferson promised to remove the Cherokees from the state.

In 1803, the United States purchased the Louisiana Territory from France. Jefferson wanted the Cherokees to move from Georgia to this new land west of the Mississippi River. By 1810, a few Cherokees had moved.

In the 1820s, Georgia tried to drive the remaining Cherokees and Creeks away. Many settlers in Georgia owned plantations. They brought enslaved

By 1821, a Cherokee named Sequoyah had invented a writing system for the Cherokee language.

people to work on these large farms. The settlers wanted to expand.

However, many Cherokees did not want to move. In 1827, they joined together to create a constitution. It divided the Cherokee Nation into eight districts. Each district would elect representatives to serve on the Cherokees' National Council.

This group would form laws and make decisions for the entire Cherokee Nation. This meant the United States could no longer form treaties with small groups of Cherokees. Instead, it would need the approval of the whole council.

Even so, settlers kept moving onto Cherokee land. And in 1828, Georgia declared that its state law applied to the Cherokees. Soon, the state would not recognize Cherokee laws. This went against the Treaty of Holston, which said the Cherokee Nation was **sovereign**. The US Supreme Court said Georgia could not do this. But Georgia ignored the court's decision.

The Indian Removal Act applied to all American Indian nations in the Southeast, such as the Creeks.

President Andrew Jackson also worked to take over more land. He helped create the Indian Removal Act. It became law in May 1830. It promised the tribes in the Southeast money and supplies to move west to an area called Indian Territory. The US government said the tribes could live in this territory forever under its protection. However, that promise was broken in the late 1800s.

CHAPTER 3

LOSING LAND

One by one, the American Indian nations in the Southeast were forced off their lands. President Jackson sent US **officials** to the Choctaws first. The Choctaw leaders refused to give up their land. But the US officials forced them to leave. The Choctaws signed the Treaty of Dancing Rabbit Creek in September 1830.

Many American Indian nations were forced to leave their land and make a hard journey west.

US officials arrested and beat anyone who refused to go.

The Choctaws began the journey west in November 1831. Some rode in wagons. Most had to walk. That winter was harsh, and the trip took much longer than people expected. Wagons got stuck, and food ran low. Cholera broke out. Many people died.

The Creeks signed the Treaty of Cusseta in March 1832. They agreed to give up part of their land to the settlers. The US government was supposed to protect the rest of the land. But the government did not stop settlers from taking it. And in 1836, the rest of the Creeks were ordered to leave. Thousands

The fighting between the Seminoles and the US soldiers lasted from 1835 to 1842.

had been forced from their homes by 1837. Once again, many people died along the way to Indian Territory.

Many Seminole leaders turned down a treaty in 1832. Three years later, fighting broke out between the Seminoles and US soldiers. This war lasted for seven years.

Many Seminoles fled to Florida. The rest surrendered. They were forced to leave their land.

The Chickasaws saw the suffering of the Seminoles. They felt they had no choice but to sell their land. Between 1837 and 1838, the Chickasaws traveled west. They were able to travel during a warmer season, so fewer people died. But it was still a difficult journey.

In 1835, a group of Cherokee leaders traveled to Washington, DC. They tried to meet with President Jackson. But Jackson refused to see them. He insisted that John Schermerhorn would handle all interactions with American Indians.

President Andrew Jackson (right) supported the removal of American Indians from their land.

In December 1835, Schermerhorn called a meeting with Cherokee leaders. The meeting was held in the Cherokee capital of New Echota, Georgia. Only a few Cherokee leaders were able to come. After several days of **negotiations**, they signed the Treaty of New Echota. They agreed to sell their land east of the Mississippi River.

JOHN ROSS

John Ross was a Cherokee leader. He was still in Washington, DC, during the meeting at New Echota. When he found out about it, he was furious. Ross and other Cherokees felt betrayed by the treaty signers. "Our hearts are sickened," Ross wrote. "We have neither land nor home, nor resting place that can be called our own."

Ross tried to stop the treaty from taking effect. He wrote a **petition** to the US Congress. He explained that the treaty signers did not have the authority to sell the land. A small group of leaders could not give up land where thousands of people lived.

Ross wrote that many Cherokees did not want to give up "our rights, our possessions, and our common country." His petition was signed by 15,000 Cherokees who did not want to move.

John Ross was the principal chief of the Cherokee Nation from 1828 to 1866.

But it did not change the US government's decision. The treaty was approved in May 1836.

CHAPTER 4

THE TRAIL OF TEARS

After the Treaty of New Echota was approved, the Cherokees were given two years to move to Indian Territory. But most refused to leave. So, in 1838, US soldiers forced them to move. Led by Major General Winfield Scott, the troops rounded up the Cherokees and forced them into waiting camps.

Some Cherokees were held at Fort Marr before they were forced to travel west.

The camps were hot and dirty. Many people died of disease. Meanwhile, white settlers looted the items that the Cherokees had left behind.

In June 1838, the soldiers began moving groups of people west. Some

RELOCATION ROUTES

NORTHERN ROUTE

IN

IL

MO

KY

N
W E
S

DISBANDMENT ROUTES

HILDEBRAND ROUTE

BENGE ROUTE

TAYLOR ROUTE

TN

DREW ROUTE

NC

BELL ROUTE

BELL-DRANE ROUTE

DRANE ROUTE

INDIAN TERRITORY

WATER ROUTE

DEAS-WHITELEY ROUTE

ROUNDUP ROUTES

AR

MS

AL

GA

groups traveled along the Tennessee River in boats. Other groups traveled over land. These groups were forced to march on foot. Wagons hauled food and supplies. Some people had to walk more than 800 miles (1,300 km).

The journey was extremely difficult. Heat, lack of water, and illness killed many people along the way. Babies and the elderly were especially at risk.

The trip was expected to take two months. But for many groups, it took as long as four months because of illness and bad weather. Many people were still marching when winter came. At night, they had to sleep on the freezing ground.

Few people had blankets. Many froze to death. Others died from pneumonia. As many as 22 people died each night.

In the morning, family members quickly buried the dead. Then they were forced to keep moving. Anyone who did not move fast enough was beaten. Because of this hardship and cruelty, the journey became known as the Trail of Tears. Between 3,000 and 4,000 Cherokees died along the way. The survivors were forced to start over in unfamiliar land. Many had lost family members along the way.

By March 1839, all five American Indian nations had been driven out of the Southeast. US settlers moved into the

A statue at the Giles County Trail of Tears Memorial in Tennessee shows the hardships the Cherokees faced.

25 million acres (10 million hectares) of land where these people once lived. Many settlers brought enslaved people to work the land. A new era of brutal slaveholding began to take root. The United States was growing and developing, but at an incredibly high cost.

FOCUS ON
THE INDIAN REMOVAL ACT AND THE TRAIL OF TEARS

Write your answers on a separate piece of paper.

1. Write a paragraph summarizing the main ideas of Chapter 1.

2. Do you think the Cherokee leaders who signed the Treaty of New Echota did the right thing? Why or why not?

3. Which US president supported the Indian Removal Act?

    A. Andrew Jackson
    B. Thomas Jefferson
    C. George Washington

4. Why did the Chickasaws agree to relocate?

    A. They would be paid a very large amount of money by the US government.
    B. They saw what happened to the Seminoles and worried it would happen to them as well.
    C. They wanted to move farther to the west where the land was better for growing crops.

Answer key on page 32.

GLOSSARY

acculturation
The process of adding to or changing the beliefs or practices that make up a group's culture.

convert
To change religions or other beliefs.

council
A group that makes decisions and rules for a larger group of people.

negotiations
Discussions that take place to reach an agreement.

officials
People who work and act for a government.

petition
A formal request sent to an official person or group.

representatives
People who speak on behalf of a larger group.

sovereign
Free to make rules and decisions without being controlled by another country.

treaty
An official agreement between groups.

TO LEARN MORE

BOOKS

Alexander, Richard. *Broken Treaties: Native American Migrations*. New York: PowerKids Press, 2016.

Klar, Jeremy, and Ann Byers. *A Primary Source Investigation of the Trail of Tears*. New York: Rosen Publishing, 2015.

Machajewski, Sarah. *The Cherokee People*. New York: Gareth Stevens Publishing, 2015.

NOTE TO EDUCATORS

Visit **www.focusreaders.com** to find lesson plans, activities, links, and other resources related to this title.

INDEX

Answer Key: 1. Answers will vary; 2. Answers will vary; 3. A; 4. B